in

THE DEADLY PRANK
AND OTHER DEVIOUS PLOTS
BOOK 1

Adapted from the original
Tinkle comics

in

THE DEADLY PRANK

AND OTHER DEVIOUS PLOTS

BOOK 1

Adapted from the original
Tinkle comics

Written by
RITUJA SAWANT

Published by
Rupa Publications India Pvt. Ltd 2023
7/16, Ansari Road, Daryaganj
New Delhi 110002

Sales centres:
Prayagraj Bengaluru Chennai
Hyderabad Jaipur Kathmandu
Kolkata Mumbai

This is a work of fiction. Names, characters, places and incidents are either the product of the author's imagination or are used fictitiously and any resemblance to any actual person, living or dead, events or locales is entirely coincidental.

P-ISBN: 978-93-5702-402-0
E-ISBN: 978-93-5520-950-4

First impression 2023

10 9 8 7 6 5 4 3 2 1

Printed in India

CONTENTS

TRUE FRIENDS

History will always remember Tantri, the trusted Mantri of Raja Hooja, as the most loyal and devoted minister in the kingdom of Hujli. There are so many stories of Tantri's brave exploits, like how he protected his beloved king from foiled devious ploys and from countless acts of treason.

What history may not talk about though, is the innumerable tales of how Tantri himself had tried – and failed – in his wicked endeavours to become the King of Hujli. He was the most committed minister of all times... committed to getting rid of Raja Hooja. While he grudgingly went about running royal errands for Raja Hooja, he plotted several creative schemes to kill the king.

One such morning, Tantri lay beaming on his balcony, enjoying a daydream. His fantasies started in different ways, in a multitude of settings, but they always ended in the same way – Raja Hooja deceased and Tantri super pleased!

This time, the daydream had an exotic setting, where Raja Hooja and Tantri were at the 'Wonders of the Bio World' exhibit. They were walking through a field of comically large Venus flytraps. Suddenly, in one swift motion, the carnivorous plant opened its trap, grabbed the king and snapped shut! And just like that, Raja Hooja became plant food and Tantri became the new king. Just as Tantri was beginning to enjoy his grand coronation, he was rudely interrupted by a loud knock.

Furious, he opened the door and barked at the royal messenger, "This better be important or I swear I am going to have you hanged!"

"Umm... apologies respected Tantriji... I did not mean to disturb you... but... but ..." the royal messenger stuttered.

"But what? Spit it out! I haven't got all day!" yelled Tantri.

"You have been summoned by His Majesty King Hooja, Master of the Seven Seas, Light of the Globe, Lord of the Universe, Ruler of Thrones, to the royal stables right away!" the royal messenger read out from his scroll, as quickly as he could.

"You mean the 'Emperor of Eternal Nonsense!'" muttered Tantri, under his breath.

"Pardon me, Your Excellency..." said the royal messenger, as he couldn't hear Tantri's mumble.

"I said I will be there shortly!" said Tantri, and slammed the door on the poor royal messenger's face.

A few minutes later, as Tantri made his way to the royal stables, he noticed Raja Hooja staring at the horses.

Deep in thought, Raja Hooja was startled by Tantri's cheerful greeting.

"Good morning, Your Majesty!"

"Oh, right! It's you, Tantri!" said Raja Hooja absent-mindedly.

"What seems to be bothering you, Sire?" asked Tantri, faking genuine concern, while thinking, *What is it now, you foolish man? What could it possibly be?*

"I was just surveying our stables and royal steeds. Somehow, there seem to be far fewer horses than before. Why is that?" questioned Raja Hooja.

"If you remember, Your Majesty, we lost two of our finest horses to the disastrous bout of horse flu last year," explained Tantri. *Unfortunately, for me, kings don't catch equine flu!* thought Tantri to himself, with a small smile.

"Ah, my memory fails me, Tantri. Thankfully, I have you by my side, to help me remember all the little things I don't, my trusted friend!" said Hooja, patting his loyal minister's back.

"It's my pleasure to be of assistance," smiled Tantri, while thinking, *And someday soon I will 'assist' you to depart forever!*

Raja Hooja interrupted Tantri's happy thoughts, "So here's what I am thinking. Our neighbouring kingdom of Dublee is currently hosting the Grand Annual Horse Fair. Tantri, I want you to go and see if we can make some suitable additions to our stables."

"Sure, Your Highness, as you wish. I will leave tomorrow morning itself," replied Tantri.

"No, no. Tomorrow will not do. You must head to the fair today itself, lest we miss out on the best horses!" insisted the king.

Tantri the Mantri, nodded in agreement and left quickly, before Raja Hooja could see him roll his eyes. He muttered to himself, "Great! Another one of his fanciful, unnecessary undertakings! One day, it will all be worth it, when I will be the King of Hujli!"

The kingdom of Dublee was not too far, and Tantri made it there by noon. It was peak summer, and the sun was blazing hot when Tantri reached the Grand Annual Horse Fair, soaked in his own sweat.

At the fair, there were horses of all shapes, sizes, breeds and colours. People had traveled from far and wide to buy and sell these majestic beasts. While the horse fair was indeed a grand affair, Tantri was too tired to care. He spotted a food stall and made a beeline for it. He bought himself some refreshing nimbu pani but before he could sip his lime juice, Tantri accidentally stepped on something mushy.

SQUELCH!

"Yikes!" exclaimed Tantri. He saw his left sandal caked in horse poop, and lost his temper. "Aargh! This whole place stinks! And as if that was not enough, now I am covered in this smelly dung. Why on Earth did Raja Hooja have to put me through this torture? I can't wait to take my revenge!"

As Tantri continued to rage, he tried to drag his foot through a patch of grass to clean out the horse dung. As he bent down to get the last bits out...

BUMP!

He toppled over and fell flat on his face into the grass.

"You brute!" he yelled, as he turned and saw a big, beautiful mare staring him down.

"Stop! Stay, Silver Streak!" shouted the stablehand, in mild panic, as she pulled hard at the reins of the mare.

"Mind your wild mare! Control her! I could have died!" scolded Tantri.

As he stood and dusted his clothes, he continued to grimace at the stablehand.

"Hahaha! If you think my sweet-tempered Silver Streak is wild, wait till you meet my Black Thunder!" replied the stablehand, cheekily.

"No, thank you. I will pass. The name sounds ominous enough," dismissed Tantri.

"Ah! But for all his dark moods, Black Thunder is by far the finest horse at the fair!" claimed the stable hand, gesturing towards the black stallion.

Black Thunder was indeed a striking horse. He was tall with a muscular body, a strong, thick neck and a lustrous black mane. Tantri was spellbound by his beauty and walked towards his enclosure for a closer look.

NEIGHHHHHH!

SNORT!

Black Thunder let out an aggressive cry.

Interesting. Very interesting, thought Tantri as a wicked grin spread across his face.

"Why don't I see any buyers lining up for such a fine horse?" enquired Tantri.

"Well... umm... that's because there is just a minor problem... But I will sell him at cost.

Honestly, that's a steal of a deal," offered the stablehand, slyly.

"At cost? Clearly you seem overly eager to get rid of this so-called prized horse!" smirked Tantri, while an evil plan was taking shape in his crafty little head.

"The fair will end tomorrow and I have to make sure I sell this horse by then. He's been on the market for some time now and is rather infamous in the horse-trading circles," shared the stablehand.

"What's his problem? Genetic? Kinetic? Gastric? Hahaha!" chuckled Tantri heartily, at his own cleverness.

"Ah well, you did not hear it from me... but Black Thunder gets really violent around men," she answered.

"Ha! There it is! No wonder you don't even have a single taker!" retorted Tantri.

But the word 'violent' had intrigued Tantri. He leaned in and asked, "When you say violent, how violent are we talking about here?"

"What do you think? The 'trample to death' kind of violent. He will mangle any man unlucky enough to get close to him!" said the stablehand, grumpily.

"Then we have a deal! I want that horse," said Tantri, with barely concealed delight.

"Huh?" cried the stablehand, in utter disbelief.

"How much for this sweet stallion?"

"One thousand Hujrees only, Your Excellency!"

"Done! Have him delivered to the royal stables of Hujli palace today itself!" ordered Tantri the Mantri.

"Wonderful! Since you have closed this deal so quickly, I would like to add a freebie – Black Thunder's friend!"

Tantri was thrilled. "Another rogue horse? Perfect! The more the merrier!" he exclaimed. *Even Raja Hooja, with his everlasting luck will find it impossible to escape two murderous horses,* thought Tantri.

"No... not a horse. It's a donkey..."

"Forget it! I am not interested in a donkey. You can keep him," snapped Tantri, dismissively.

The stablehand was about to say something, but stopped herself. She had finally managed to sell this rampaging horse; there was no point in sabotaging the deal, she decided.

Tantri handed her a bag of one thousand Hujrees and walked away. He was pleased with the way this trip had turned out after all, and made his way back to the palace happily.

The next morning, Tantri woke up with a big, fat grin. "Today is my day... My throne awaits! I shall be king, without further delay..." Tantri sang to himself, while he wore his lucky turban.

Raja Hooja was out in the royal gardens, enjoying his early morning laddoos. Tantri walked up to him, thinking, *That's right, Hungry Hooja! Enjoy your last laddoo. The clock is ticking! Tee-hee!*

"Good morning, Your Majesty! I have an excellent surprise for you!" said Tantri, giddy with excitement.

"Surprise? Oh Tantri, you have just made my day! You know, how much I love surprises!" said Raja Hooja, looking pleased.

"This surprise is a special gift for my special king. I just can't wait to show it to you," flattered Tantri.

"Enough with the suspense. Give it to me already!" ordered Raja Hooja.

"As you please, Your Highness. It's only a short walk away," gestured Tantri towards the walking path.

"Walk? Now? But it's just after dawn!"

"It's the perfect time, Sire. Golden hour and all," urged Tantri the Mantri.

Also, it's the perfect hour to get rid of you! It's early enough to have fewer spectators for my deathly surprise, thought Tantri.

"Sure, sure. Let's walk,' replied Raja Hooja, standing up reluctantly, but still eager to see his gift.

As they went towards the royal stables, Raja Hooja looked joyful, "Ah Tantri, there seems to be a new horse enclosure, that means... let me guess, you have got me a brand-new horse!"

Tantri merely smiled, while he sarcastically thought to himself, *Applause! Give this man a medal for his genius detective skills!*

"You are just so clever, Your Majesty. It's impossible to hide any surprises from you!" said Tantri.

"I know, I know. I don't mean to brag, but my mother, Her Royal Highness, always said that I was the cleverest Hooja ever born!"

That's not saying much, given that all your ancestors were even bigger dunderheads than you! But I intend to end this line today with my evil, genius plan, sniggered Tantri to himself.

As they neared Black Thunder's enclosure, Tantri suddenly stopped.

Raja Hooja turned back and asked, "What's the matter Tantri? Why are you stopping?"

Tantri needed to stay out of harm's way. "I will wait right here, Your Highness. As you are well aware, I am always uneasy around animals," said Tantri, sheepishly.

"Uneasy? You mean, super scared! You are always running away from dogs and horses. Even in our Gurukul days, remember you were chased by a gaggle of geese?" Raja Hooja had a hearty laugh.

HAHAHA!

As if your taunts will ever let me forget such traumatic childhood tales. You laugh now, but I will have the last laugh today, thought Tantri, while pretending to laugh along.

"All right, Tantri. It's time to watch and learn. See how I show them who's the boss," said Raja Hooja, as he confidently walked through the gates.

Tantri called out, "It will be my absolute pleasure, Your Majesty..."

"... to watch your end!" mumbled the evil Mantri, softly under his breath.

Raja Hooja abruptly stopped in his tracks and turned, "Oh! I almost forgot. I also have a surprise for you, Tantri. And it's right here in the stables."

"How thoughtful, Your Highness. Perhaps we can look at my surprise after yours. I am so eager to see your reaction," urged Tantri.

"Tantri, my dear friend. You spoil your king with all these gifts. And somehow all your gifts are so unusual..." Raja's Hooja's voice trailed off, as he walked into the stables.

This is it! It's all in your hands or should I say hooves now, Black Thunder. Teehee! thought Tantri, gleefully.

NEIGHHHHHH!
NEIGHHHHHHH!

Attaboy! thought Tantri as he fell into a happy daydream, where he was picking out fancy royal robes for his grand coronation ceremony.

Meanwhile, inside the enclosure, Raja Hooja saw his gift, Black Thunder, and was charmed by his majestic beauty.

"There you are, my sweet stallion. Aren't you simply stunning," smiled Raja Hooja, as he gently approached the horse.

Black Thunder walked slowly and neighed softly, as the king lovingly patted his neck. Tantri waited on the other side of the gate, to hear Raja Hooja holler for help!

NEIGHHHHHH!
THUDUKTHUDUKTHUDUK!
CRASH!

Oh, that sounds brutal, thought Tantri, as he decided to walk away.

But then, there was surprisingly another loud sound...

HEEHAW! HEEHAW!

HEEHAW!

"Huh? Do horses bray when they charge at humans?" asked Tantri, as he cautiously opened the gate to sneak a peek at the ongoing mayhem.

He was met with the most baffling sight! The side fence was broken, indicating where a donkey had entered. And instead of charging murderously at Raja Hooja, Black Thunder was nuzzling the donkey! The scene looked full of love and not at all like the planned murder scene.

Looking at Tantri's bewildered expression, Raja Hooja offered an explanation, "By the way, Tantri meet Bottom, the donkey. I bought him as a present, especially for you, from the horse fair."

Tantri was appalled! *He bought a donkey for me at a horse fair. How typical,* he thought.

Raja Hooja continued, "You know, his owner said that he had stopped eating, as someone had bought his friend – a real hothead who charged at anyone he saw."

"But this horse looks..." started Tantri.

Raja Hooja interrupted, "But the same hothead of a horse turned as meek as a mouse in Bottom's company. Can you believe that?"

No, I cannot! I cannot believe that my feral plan has turned into a friendly reunion. Bah! Tantri lamented, silently.

"And Tantri, look at the coincidence! You and I bought the horse and the donkey for each other. Now that's true friendship for you! Just like ours!" grinned Hooja, as he hugged his true friend, Tantri the Mantri.

True friendship, my foot! More like a never-ending

enemyship! thought Tantri as he accepted his defeat.

And so, yet another one of Tantri's elaborate schemes to wipe out his beloved enemy, failed miserably.

THE TUMBLING STATUES

It was a bright, clear and sunny morning in Hujli. Raju, a young sculptor, was busy in his studio, and had begun his work day with a literal bang.

"A perfect day for carving yet another masterpiece," said Raju, smugly to himself as he continued to chisel away at a large block of marble.

Meanwhile, Tantri the Mantri was out and about, running yet another futile errand for Raja Hooja.

The king wanted his favourite minister to personally ensure an uninterrupted supply of sweetmeats for the upcoming royal feast.

"Not a day goes by when I don't have to waste my precious time trying to satisfy Hooja's cravings," grumbled Tantri.

Suddenly, he was startled by a loud sound...

CRASHHHHH!

He looked up and saw a sign – 'Sculptor's Studio'. But what made him stop right in his tracks were the words a man was yelling from inside the studio.

"Not this AGAIN! This is the fourth time this week and it's only Wednesday! Your statues are a DEATH TRAP!"

Death Trap! That's all Tantri needed to hear. He couldn't stop the evil smile that appeared on his face. He briskly made his way towards the studio.

How interesting... Maybe my morning doesn't need to be dull after all. I must find out more, thought Tantri.

As Tantri entered Sculptor's Studio, he heard more angry yelling.

"Raju, you are a talented and a highly experienced sculptor, but your statues always collapse like a pack of cards. How does it keep happening? Enough is enough. This will not do, not do at all!"

"Excuse me," Tantri interrupted.

The master sculptor and Raju both looked at Tantri, who was now walking across the studio towards them. Sculptor's Studio was filled with beautiful freestanding statues of all different shapes and sizes, carved out of a variety of stones. A bunch of chisels and hammers were neatly laid out on a wooden table, near the window. A large heap of crushed stones was lying in the middle of the room.

"What seems to be the problem here, Masterji?" asked Tantri.

"Mantriji, Raju's sculptures look sturdy, but they keep collapsing due to their weak bases. It is said that great sculptures can roll down a hill without breaking, but his can break a hill! It's lucky no one was standing near this one or else they would not have survived. We work with very heavy stones, after all, and this can be so dangerous," he complained, as he pointed at the rubble.

This was music to Tantri's ears. He was delighted and had a special offer for Raju.

"This young sculptor seems to be exceptionally talented... in just the right way. I need his services for a very special project. I would love to commission a unique statue created by him, and him alone!" said Tantri, gleefully.

The bewildered master sculptor accepted the advance from Tantri and thanked him for the order. "You will receive the picture for the statue tomorrow morning. I want this ready before the royal feast!"

few weeks later, at the royal palace of Huji, preparations were in full swing for a grand royal feast to celebrate the Founder's Day. Raja Hooja and his trusted Tantri the Mantri were inspecting the decorations, when a royal messenger came up to them and announced, "Excuse me, Tantriji. The new statue that you ordered, will be delivered to the palace by tomorrow morning."

"What statue? Tantri, what's this about a statue?" enquired Raja Hooja.

"It was meant to be a surprise, Your Majesty. I placed an order with Sculptor's Studio for a special statue of our illustrious king — Raja Bhooja. Such a noble ruler," praised Tantri. "You've ordered a statue of my grandfather? But why?" asked Raja Hooja.

"It is only because of him that our kingdom is so... so... er... umm... blessed to have a great monarch like you!" said Tantri, with a sly smile.

I am becoming so good at flattery, I could write a book on the subject, thought Tantri to himself.

"So true. So true," agreed Raja Hooja, nodding solemnly.

Flattery gets you everywhere, especially with a pompous king, thought Tantri, with a small smile.

"But there is also another reason I ordered the statue, Your Majesty. It is made from a rare and special stone that gives out an invisible vapour, which is known to prolong life. Now isn't that something? Nothing but the best for my king," added Tantri.

"Prolongs life, you say?" asked Raja Hooja.

"Oh yes, Your Highness! Anyone with royal lineage who spends just 15 minutes near it each day will be blessed with a really long and healthy life, of at least 120 years or more!"

"120 years! Just imagine the number of laddoos I could savour in that kind of time!" chuckled Raja Hooja.

"But, of course!" agreed Tantri, trying to hide his eye-roll.

While Raja Hooja started daydreaming about his laddoo count, Tantri quickly added, "You can have your daily afternoon tea and laddoos at a special table set up right below the statue. How does that sound, Your Majesty?"

"That sounds like an immortal idea!" giggled Raja Hooja.

Now that the wicked Mantri had convinced his naive king about this high tea arrangement, he needed to make sure that his plan was foolproof, so that no one would suspect any foul play when the statue crumbled and crushed Raja Hooja to his death. So, Tantri had yet another devious thought.

"I have a splendid idea, Your Majesty! Since the statue will be installed within sight of the main gate, crowds will gather to catch a glimpse of their beloved king each afternoon. If you think it appropriate, Your Highness, we could charge a tiny fee for the Royal Darshan," suggested the poker-faced Tantri.

"My trusted Mantri, you think of everything! That money could be used for the upkeep of the palace. You know, everything is always falling apart around here," said an excited Raja Hooja.

"Falling apart... what an apt phrase, Sire!"

smiled Tantri, pleased with how his day had turned around.

"So, it's decided then. Let's start a 120-year long tradition of 'The Royal Darshan', starting this Founder's Day where your subjects get a glimpse of the great Raja Hooja," declared Tantri, with a slight bow of his head.

And all those feet walking around will also shake up the statue enough to help it 'fall apart', thought a delighted Tantri.

Soon, it was Founder's Day and Tantri could barely contain his excitement. He wore his finest robes and lucky turban. He was dressed to the nines for his special day – The Founder's Day – the beginning of a new reign in Hujli, starting with him ascending the throne.

The celebrations were afoot and crowds were beginning to collect at the main gate of the royal palace. The grand statue of Raja Bhooja was in place and Raja Hooja was all set to inaugurate

the new tradition of, 'The Royal Darshan'. Raja Hooja made his way towards his grandfather's statue to the cheering and chanting of the crowds, "Long live the king! Long live the king!"

He climbed on a long ladder and honoured the statue with a marigold garland. Tantri looked on hopefully, as he stood at a safe distance, outside the radius of destruction of the

soon-to-be tumbling statue. But, nothing happened and the afternoon went off smoothly. No crack, no creak, and definitely no crumble! The only things that crumbled were the laddoos on Raja Hooja's plate.

The following afternoon was also the same. In fact, the whole week passed uneventfully. Tantri got desperate. He had yet another wicked idea. He hired drummers to play and beat their drums loudly, hoping that the vibrations would shake up the base of the statue and help it tumble.

DHUM!

DHISH!

Raja Hooja did his customary bow to the statue and proceeded to relish his tea and snacks right below it.

Much to Tantri's dismay, despite the drummers, the statue stood as firm as rock. He just couldn't understand it.

While Tantri was losing his patience, Raja Hooja was loving his afternoon tea sessions amongst such fanfare. One evening, when the cheering crowds had left for the day, Raja Hooja called for Tantri, "My dear Mantri, I wanted to thank you for arranging this fabulous Royal Darshan. I am absolutely enjoying my afternoon tea time."

"Happy to be of service, Sire!" replied Tantri, ever so gloomily.

"Oh, by the way, I received this letter from the sculptor, Raju, the one who built my grandfather's new..."

Tantri had a lump in his throat, afraid that his death trap had been revealed. He quickly interrupted the king, "What? W-what did he say?"

"Just that he had also built two other statues for the palace, in the past."

"Two others? Really? Which ones?" asked Tantri, feeling relieved that there was no mention of any weak bases.

"One is in the infirmary, the one of my beloved grand uncle. And the other is of the founder of my dynasty – Raja Tooja!"

"Really? I didn't know this. Where is that one installed?" asked Tantri, eagerly.

"You are standing right under it, Tantri," answered Raja Hooja, pointing just behind Tantri.

"W-w-what? This one?" asked Tantri the Mantri, as he slowly turned to look up at Raja Tooja's statue.

Just as the words left his mouth, there was a strange rumbling sound.

"What's that noise?" asked a bewildered Raja Hooja, stepping away from the statue.

PLONK!
DHUB!

Tantri wasn't quick enough. Raja Tooja's heavy, stone head fell right on Tantri's light, bony one. Poor Tantri landed straight in the royal infirmary.

As he slowly regained consciousness, he groaned loudly in pain. Tantri was grumpy and disheveled.

"Where am I?" he asked, as he lay in the hospital bed. He glanced to his right and saw Raja Hooja, by his bedside, looking very concerned.

"I am so glad to see you conscious, my dear Tantri! You had me so worried. I thought I had lost you forever. In fact, I had even decided to honour your memory by getting your statue made by the very same sculptor who made my grandfather's sculpture," expressed Raja Hooja.

"How thoughtful, Your Majesty," said Tantri, sarcastically, noticing how hale and hearty the king looked.

"You must be starving, Tantri. Let's get some food into you!" said Raja Hooja. He stepped out to inform the doctor that his Mantri was finally awake.

By now, Tantri had reached the end of his patience and snapped, "Enough is enough! I will be done with you, once and for all!"

He got out of bed as fast as he could, limped out of the room behind Raja Hooja, and intended to push him down the stairs and finish him off.

But, right at that moment, just as Tantri was about to shove the king, the statue placed in the infirmary came crashing down on them both. The duo tumbled down the stairs with Tantri hugging the king.

CRASH!

While Raja Hooja escaped with a just few scratches, an already battered Tantri bore the brunt of the tumbling statue. The infirmary doctors rushed to their aid but not before Tantri had started to see stars.

"Look! Look what Tantri's done!" Tantri heard someone shout, though he was still in a dazed state. He thought his act was up and that he had been caught. As the stones were lifted off of him, he felt someone hold his arms and pull him up.

I am done for, Tantri thought as he closed his eyes and accepted his fate.

"The brave Tantri saved you, Your Highness! He pushed you away just as your grand uncle's statue came crashing down. Otherwise..." the horrified doctor's voice trailed off.

Loud cheers broke out! Everyone mistook Tantri's devilry as an act of bravery and applauded his sacrifice.

"Oh, my dear Tantri. My fearless Mantri! What would I do without you?" Raja Hooja expressed his gratitude, as Tantri groaned in agony.

A few weeks later, Raja Hooja declared Tantri as a national hero, in honour of his bravery and continued loyalty. He even had a magnificent statue of Tantri installed in the Hall of Heroes.

Everyone went to see it but to date, Tantri the Mantri has never set foot in there. He also swore off statues forever!

THE DEADLY PRANK

One lazy afternoon at the palace, Tantri the Mantri was feeling very poetic. He decided to pen down his thoughts.

Ruling over the kingdom of Hujli,
Sitting on the throne with my crown,
Living life in the lap of luxury,
Helps turn my frown upside down.

My joy truly knows no bounds,
Ever since Raja Hooja departed,
My praises flood the palace grounds,
As Tantri's reign has started.

All hail Tantri, All hail...

A loud and urgent knock on the door broke his flow.

"Ugh! What now!" muttered Tantri, as he grumpily opened the door and saw a panicked royal guard waiting there.

"Hurry! Please hurry, Mantriji! His Majesty... The Light of the Globe... The Master of the Universe... The Lord of..."

"Yes, yes! What about him?" asked Tantri, very irritably.

"His Highness, Raja Hooja, has suddenly taken ill. Seriously ill," replied the worried royal guard.

"What? How? When?" asked Tantri, a little too eagerly.

"The royal physician just informed us that the king is on his deathbed. His Majesty has summoned you to his royal bedchambers immediately. Make haste, Sire!" urged the royal guard.

Ha! There is no way I am going to miss this! I have been waiting for this day, for years, thought Tantri. He immediately rushed to Raja Hooja's bedside.

Inside the king's bedroom, Tantri was met with a scene from his dreams!

Raja Hooja lay on his lavish bed, looking deathly pale, with his eyelids shut, gasping for breath.

Holding back a smile, Tantri feigned concern, "Oh, my dear king! I never thought I would live to see this dreadful day! This is awful."

But I surely hoped to. Tee-hee, thought Tantri, with delight.

Just then, the royal attendant entered, bowed his head and announced, "Your Majesty, the finance minister, Mantri Todaji, wishes to pay his last respects to you. Should I escort him in?"

However, before the dying king could respond, Tantri butted in.

"Shoo! Do not disturb the king with such trivial requests. Can't you see, His Highness, our dear Raja Hooja, is at death's door. Now is not a good time to entertain visitors. Ask the guards to show him out immediately," said Tantri, dismissing the request.

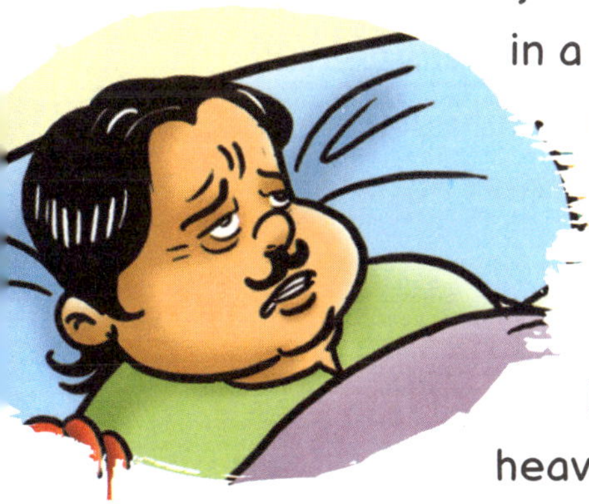

But Raja Hooja spoke slowly, in a weak voice, "No, no. Please, let him come in. I wish to meet my loyal subjects before I leave for my heavenly abode."

Ha! You really think you will gain entry into heaven after making my life this miserable? thought Tantri, with a smirk.

Mantri Todaji walked in with a get-well-soon gift, looking extremely sad, "Your Majesty, you have ruled over Hujli with kindness and wisdom for so many years. This is a small token of love from your loyal subjects. All of us are praying for your speedy recovery."

Well, not all of us. Some of us are praying for an expeditious exit, thought Tantri, looking hopeful.

"Thank you. It's been my pleasure entirely..." King Hooja's voice trailed off.

After Mantri Todaji had left the room, Raja Hooja turned towards Tantri with half-open eyes and said, "My trusted friend, I wanted to share something

important with you. Even though my life is coming to an end, I want to make sure the peace in my kingdom continues well after I am gone..."

Don't worry, you go right ahead and drop dead! There will be peace and only peace once you are gone forever, thought Tantri, looking outwardly pensive, while hiding a small smile.

"... My lawyer, Mr Golu, should be here any minute." Raja Hooja paused, gasping for breath. "I have a huge favour to ask of you, Tantri," finished Raja Hooja. Every word seemed like a huge effort.

"Anything for you, my Sire!" replied Tantri, while thinking, *Absolutely anything to get rid of you faster!*

But before Raja Hooja could say another word more, Mr Golu entered the royal bedchambers.

The dying king looked at his lawyer and instructed, "Before I leave my mortal body behind, I wish to handover the reigns of my kingdom to my most loyal and trusted minister, advisor and friend – Tantri,"

"W-what!" exclaimed Tantri the Mantri, his heart racing with joy.

"As you wish, Your Royal Highness. Please sign here for the transfer of the kingdom of Hujli," replied Mr Golu.

"Oh, no! You can't leave us, Your Majesty," sighed Tantri, while thinking, *Not before you finish all the paperwork!*

Once Raja Hooja had finished signing the documents, Mr Golu took his leave.

With crocodile tears in his eyes, Tantri sat by his bedside and said, "This is just too soon, Your Highness. If my wishes could come true, then I would wish that you could come back to life. But alas, that can never happen!"

GASP! GASP!

The king began to pant as he uttered his last words, "Goodbye, my dear friend... It's time to..."

"The king is dead! Long live the new king!" said Tantri, appearing grief-stricken and

teary-eyed, while cheerily thinking, *Boo-hoo! Have a happy afterlife!*

Before Tantri could start to truly celebrate, Mr Golu promptly reappeared and offered Mantriji his condolences, "My deepest sympathy for your loss. King Hooja's demise must be really hard on you. But the people of Hujli need their new king now. So, from tomorrow, you will have to assume your royal duties and responsibilities as the King of Hujli, Your Highness."

"Of course, I will spend my life in the service of my loyal subjects," replied Tantri, sounding earnest and drifting into a daydream...

And finally, I can create the kingdom of my dreams... where the rich will never pay any taxes... just a special "Tantri Tax"... where I will cut down the forests of Hujli to make way for state-of-the-art factories and make enormous profits... where the people of Hujli can toil away day and night, so that I can swim

in a pool of pure gold... ! thought a starry-eyed Tantri.

"Ahem! Excuse me, Tantri... Umm... Your Highness... The royal bedchambers have been prepared for you. Please get some rest now. Tomorrow is a big day!" advised the lawyer, with a slight bow before his new king.

"Huh? Oh, yes, yes," said Tantri, as he was jolted back to reality.

Tantri started to fall asleep lying on the softest mattress with the most luxurious silky sheets. After all these years of wanting to be the king, it was finally his time to live life king-size. He was the King of Hujli!

Just as he was falling into a deep and peaceful slumber, he heard an eerie sound...

HOO! HOO! HOOOOOOO!

"Huh, what's that? Who's there?" gulped Tantri.

Suddenly, the windows swung open and the door slammed shut, as a strong gust of cold wind blew in.

"W-what! Who, who opened the windows?" yelled a spooked Tantri.

WHOOSH! WHOOSH!

"Who is it? Show yourself!" cried Tantri, helplessly.

What the newly minted king saw next, chilled him to the bone. A ghastly figure, dressed in

all white, stood in the window, holding a candle. The glow of the flame lit its face – which was jet black with only narrow glowing slits for eyes. It was a truly sinister sight. Tantri was absolutely terrified.

"It's me, Hoooooooooja. I miss youuuuuu, Tantri, my friend. It's very lonely up there. Come, join meeeeee," the terrifying ghost said, in a creepy voice.

"Hoo... hoo... Hooja's ghost! He's here to haunt me... Aaaaaaaaaaaaa," screamed Tantri, as he sprang out of bed and made a dash towards the door.

EEEEEEEEEEEEE!

A shrill shriek echoed through the corridors as Tantri ran to save his poor soul.

"Guards! Come here at once! Your king summons you!" Tantri frantically screamed.

But nobody came. The palace was eerily quiet and mysteriously unlit. In the pitch-dark of the night, while he was feeling for a light switch, Tantri found a phone. He put it to his ear, but all he heard was the same scary 'hoo' sound.

"Somebody! Anybody! HELP ME!" Tantri continued to wail, but to no avail.

"Is everyone here dead?" screamed Tantri.

"Not everyone... Just me... my dear Tantriiiii," replied the creepy voice.

Unnerved, poor Tantri darted across the palace gardens and ran for his life.

HOO! HOO! HOOOOOOO!

Just as Tantri was sprinting towards the palace gates, he heard a voice.

"Stop! Don't run, Tantri."

"Noooooo way! Get away from me!" shrieked Tantri.

"Wait! It's just me, your king – Hooja!" Raja Hooja shouted from the palace terrace.

"J-just you! A very dead you!" replied Tantri.

"Guards! Stop him!" Raja Hooja instructed the royal guards at the main gate.

"Please save me from that ghost! Let me out! I don't want to be the king anymore! Just let me out!" pleaded Tantri, now panting.

HAHAHA!

But instead of helping him, the royal guards just laughed hysterically.

"Huh! What is WRONG with everyone?" demanded Tantri.

"Bring him to me!" commanded Raja Hooja.

Resigned to his fate, Tantri let the guards escort him to Raja's Hooja's ghost. The palace lights were back on and when Tantri

saw Raja Hooja, he did not look translucent like a usual ghost. He looked quite solid like a real, living, breathing person.

"Your Highness, how are you back from the dead?" asked Tantri, perplexed.

"Oh, silly Tantri! I never died in the first place. This was all an elaborate prank. Hahaha!" replied Raja Hooja.

But Tantri was not amused, "This is so not fair! How could you play such a deadly prank on me?"

"Well... I probably did take it a tad too far. But today is the first of April. All is fair on April fool's day and I decided to prank my favourite mantri!" said Raja Hooja, cheerfully.

"Bah! But what about Mr Golu and all the signed documents?" asked Tantri, grumpily.

"Golu, the lawyer, is my childhood friend. We were simply the best pranksters. So, we decided to revive our old April fool's day tradition and relive our childhood memories. But you must admit, my dear Tantri, that we spooked you for good. Hahaha!"

"Indeed!" agreed Tantri, grudgingly. *You laugh now, but someday soon I will have the last laugh!* he thought.

PAST SAVING

Every Sunday, Tantri the Mantri had a weekly ritual. He would sit with a cup of hot tea and rusk, reading the newspaper from cover to cover. He loved catching up on all the important matters that had transpired in Hujli. While he was enjoying a leisurely morning, he saw his wife, Hoki, grabbing her purse and sandals.

"Where are you off to in such a hurry, Hoki?" asked Tantri, as he bit into his rusk and took a sip of tea.

"Oh, I am running so late! No time to talk, Tantri," replied Hoki, as she hastily slipped on her sandals.

"Yes, but late for what?" asked Tantri, biting into a crunchy piece of rusk.

"I'd told you! You forgot? There's a grand convention today as the famous witch guru is in town," replied Hoki, incredulously.

"Which Guru? What Guru?" asked Tantri, curiously.

"Not what guru... WITCH guru! Mystica! She is only the most influential of all the witches! Every year she visits different places to

spread her extensive knowledge and healing," replied Hoki.

"Spellbound, are we? Tee-hee," chuckled Tantri, at his own joke.

Hoki rolled her eyes. "Never mind, I have got to run. I don't want to be late and miss meeting the most powerful witch of all time!" said Hoki, stepping out of the front door.

At the mention of the words 'most powerful', Tantri's ears perked up.

"Wait! She's the most powerful, you say? Then I must meet her too!" said Tantri, with an evil grin.

To Tantri's surprise, the Witches' Convention was a fancy affair and the auditorium was packed with an excited audience. Suddenly, the hall went dim and quiet as everyone stared at the stage in anticipation.

WHOOSH!

From a mystical green cloud of smoke, emerged a tall, wise witch wearing an

outlandish outfit. She smiled at the thundering applause and when she spoke, there was pin drop silence.

"Welcome, my dear friends! I am Mystica. Welcome to an enchanting experience with me. Let's make magic!"

Tantri was amused by the grand entrance and very skeptical. He sniggered. Hoki jabbed him with her elbow and whispered, "Shhh! Be quiet!"

"Is she supposed to be the 'all-powerful' witch of 'all-time'? You can't be serious! Just look at her. She's dressed like a green, leafy cabbage. Such Hokum!" sneered Tantri.

HOKUM...HOKUM...

Tantri's voice echoed in the auditorium and promptly reached Mystica's ears.

"Oh, no!" cringed Hoki, as she sank into her seat in embarrassment.

"Well, well, well! It would seem we have a non-believer amongst us today. What's your name, my dear fellow? Come, join me up here," announced Mystica, gesturing towards the stage.

Tantri the Mantri rudely ignored the invitation and instead replied arrogantly, "Since you are the all-knowing, most powerful witch guru, surely you must already know who I am, Miss Mystica!"

"But of course! You must be that snooty royal minister of Hujli," replied Mystica, haughtily, with a small smile.

"That was just a lucky guess. Any common charlatan could have done that!" said Tantri the Mantri, cheekily.

At this insult, Mystica got disgusted with the conceited minister and decided to teach him a lesson. She closed her eyes and with an outstretched palm, muttered a spell.

ZZZAAAPPP!

In the blink of an eye, Tantri was floating mid-air above his seat, in a light, shimmering, wavy bubble.

GASP!

Hoki and the entire audience gulped in awe and shock. But Tantri was unfazed.

He threatened Mystica, "How dare you! I am Tantri the Mantri, Raja Hooja's most trusted minister! You have made a grave mistake by unseating me from my throne... I mean my chair! Put me down! At once!"

"Very proud of our high post in the kingdom, are we? Let's send you where you have no kingdom!" said Mystica, with a snap of her fingers.

And just like that, Tantri vanished from the floating, wavy bubble, and disappeared out of the convention.

He reappeared, of course. Just not in the same place... or in the same time!

"Huh! What just happened? Where am I?" cried Tantri, looking around frantically for Hoki or Mystica or the auditorium.

He found himself in the wilderness, surrounded by tall trees, standing on a muddy slope by the bank of a river.

"Aaaaaaaaah! Where did that awful witch send me?" he yelled at the tree next to him.

He ran around in a panicked state, calling out for help, "Hello! Hello! Is there anyone here? I need to get back to Hujli urgently. Hellooooo?" But all he heard in response was the chirping of birds and the gushing of the river.

Meanwhile, back at the auditorium, a very worried Hoki gathered all her courage and approached Mystica backstage, after the lecture. She said, "Umm... Madam Mystica! Please, I need your help."

"Hoki! How good to see you, my dear. How have you been?"

"Err... I have been good but I can't say the same for my husband. He is the one you sent off somewhere else... I'm sorry about his behaviour... Can you please bring him back?" requested Hoki.

"Oh, him! I forgot all about him! You are married to that rude minister? How unfortunate. Anyway,

I have sent him to a special place... or should I say a special time in the past... when the kingdom of Hujli hadn't been formed yet... just to give him a taste of what it is like to be without his royal privileges," replied Mystica, looking thoughtful.

"I am sure he has learned his lesson... I need him to come back to me..." pleaded Hoki, looking rather sad.

"All right, all right! Don't fret, Hoki. I will give you the spell and the list of ingredients required to bring him back. You will be able to recall him by yourself. But the spell will take a few hours to work," said Mystica, as she started writing on a sheet of paper.

Hoki thanked her and heaved a sigh of relief.

Meanwhile, our poor Tantri, sat down gloomily, in the distant past, considering his options. He looked around and thought to himself, *No Raja Hooja to plot against, no Hujli to covet and no*

Hoki to chat with. Now what am I supposed to do with all of my time?

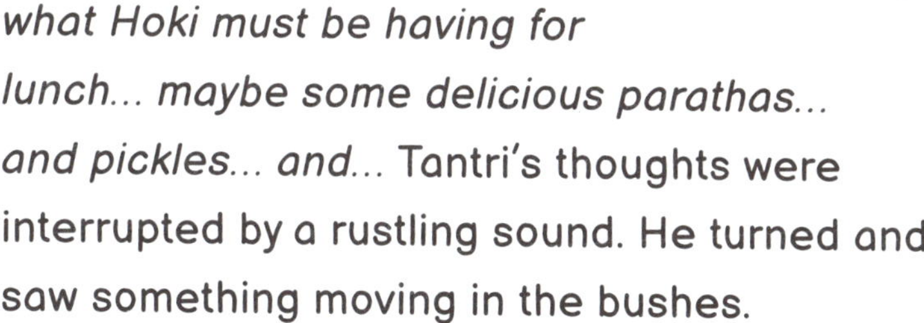

He was getting hungry and decided to go around foraging for some fruits. *I wonder what Hoki must be having for lunch... maybe some delicious parathas... and pickles... and...* Tantri's thoughts were interrupted by a rustling sound. He turned and saw something moving in the bushes.

"This is it! This is how it all ends. I become someone's lunch while looking for my own!" lamented Tantri.

MOOOOOOOOO!

Tantri blinked his eyes in surprise. There, right in

front of him, was the strangest sight. A jolly cow, with a man completely passed out, lying across its back was slowly emerging from the bushes. "Huh! W-what! Is that a cow? And with a rider, no less. Finally, a human. I am not alone... I am not alone!" celebrated Tantri, as he jumped up and down with joy.

He rushed to the cow and nudged the man riding it. But he did not budge. Tantri raised his face and saw that the man was fast asleep, snoring. He somehow lifted the heavy man off the cow's back and made him lie down on the ground.

Tantri splashed handfuls of water from the river on the sleeping man's face.

SPLASH!

"Ackkk! Baaaa! Baaaa!" shouted the alarmed stranger, as he woke up.

"Huh? Hello? Do you speak 'Sheep'?" asked a baffled Tantri. *Drat! A Sheep-human? There go my chances of getting saved!* thought Tantri, glumly.

"Hahaha! No-no. I don't speak 'Sheep'. Earlier today, I just lost my sheep. I set out in search of them and must have fallen asleep on Moo," answered the shepherd, smiling at Tantri.

"Moo?"

"Moo is the name of my cow. The one who is currently munching on the back of your kurta," said the shepherd, pointing towards Tantri's torn kurta.

EEEEK! SHOO, MOO!

"Please, pardon her manners, Sir! She's just hungry and we have had a really long day with no food. Our village was hit by a storm and then my scared sheep wandered away. Moo and I have been looking for them, both of us on empty stomachs, since morning. Nothing is more important than food, I always say," said the shepherd.

Something about this shepherd seemed oddly familiar to Tantri. But his thoughts were interrupted by some loud cries.

HELP! HELP! PLEASE HELP US!

Tantri, the shepherd and Moo, all rushed towards the sounds which were coming from the river. There, they saw a whole bunch of people struggling to stay afloat, bobbing up and down, screaming to be saved.

"Oh! Those poor people are from my village! I was afraid they had perished in the storm. Sir, we have to find a way to save them!" urged the shepherd, desperately looking at Tantri for a solution.

"Chief! Is that you?! You are alive! Please save us!" begged a drowning woman.

"Chief! Save our souls!" chanted another, as they were slowly floating away from the bank of the river.

"Chief! Help us!" yelled a third.

"Chief? Are you their chief?" asked a bemused Tantri, while thinking, *Ugh! Here I was thinking he was a shepherd! He's a chief! Even this clown can become a 'Chief' but someone as clever as me is yet to be king.*

"Yes, yes. I am Chief Tooja, the village head.

How should we save them?" responded Chief Tooja, looking around frantically for some way to help his people.

In all this chaos, Tantri's mind was racing. Turning a dreadful threat into an opportunity for himself was his unique talent.

Hmm... Now that I am stuck here in this random village, I need a new life plan. If I rescue these moaning mortals, I can contest this Tooja for the title of village chief. When I rescue these villagers, they will owe me. Who knows, maybe I can even start a brand-new kingdom and become their king. Tee-hee! thought Tantri with a wicked smile.

"I have an excellent idea!" Tantri announced loudly, while staring intently at a partly-broken tree on the edge of the river.

"What is it? What are we going to do?" asked Chief Tooja, eagerly.

"Just watch and learn!" said Tantri, walking towards Moo, who was still happily chewing away on the piece of cloth that she had managed to rip away from Tantri's kurta.

Tantri went up to the cow and tugged at the cloth inside her mouth but she held on. He tugged again, harder this time and yanked the cloth from Moo's mouth.

GRR! MOOOOOOOOOO!

The angered bovine charged at Tantri, who held

out the chewed-up piece of cloth right in front of the broken tree.

BAM! CRACK! SPLASH!

With one mighty headbutt, Moo had managed to break the tree trunk. And, just as Tantri had planned, it fell across the river. All the villagers were able to climb ashore with the help of the fallen log.

"It worked! It worked!" applauded Chief Tooja, as he helped the villagers get back on their feet.

"Long live Chief Tooja! Long live Chief Tooja!" cheered all the survivors.

But Chief Tooja was a fair man and gave credit where credit was due, "No, no, my dear people! This had nothing to do with me. It was all him. It was my friend here who helped me and saved all of you!"

"Hello! My name is Tantri and it was my pleasure to save all your lives," said Tantri, gloating away.

"You helped our Chief Tooja? You must be a wise man!" said a villager.

"Yes, yes. You are wise and mighty," praised the second.

"Maybe you could be our chief?" added a third.

Tantri, who was feeling full of himself, took charge and said, "Settle down, settle down. I know what you all are thinking. Since all of you have lost your homes and village to this

terrible storm, you are all looking for a fresh start. I think it's time to build a new life for all of us right here... in a new kingdom. I hereby establish this land as the new kingdom of Hujli," declared Tantri, looking extremely pleased.

Because that's the only kingdom I have ever wanted, thought Tantri to himself, with a smug smile.

Chief Tooja swiftly chimed in, "Yes! A new kingdom is a great idea! And I quite like the sound of Hujli. My dear people, as your chief, I will be happy to be your new king!"

Ha! Now I know who this Chief Tooja reminds me of... a certain annoying king back home who refuses to die, thought Tantri.

"Hold your horses, Chief Tooja. New kingdom, new rules. How about a vote? We can let the people choose their ruler," suggested Tantri the Mantri, feeling confident that the villagers would pick him – their saviour.

Everyone, including Chief Tooja, agreed on a vote and the villagers stepped away to discuss their choices. Shortly after, they came back with the announcement, "Our decision has been unanimous and we all agree that our new king is—"

POOF!

WHA—!

NOOOOOOOOO!

In that exact moment, Tantri got pulled back into the present day Hujli, and reappeared before Hoki, who was chanting a spell, in their living room.

"Hoki! No! What did you do?" cried Tantri, in utter disbelief.

"Not a word from you, Tantri! You always make a mess and I am left cleaning up after you. I have had enough for today. I am done.

Good night!" replied Hoki, leaving the room crossly.

"B-but, wait! What about my Hujli? I was finally going to be the 'King of Hujli'. No-no! This cannot be real. I need to go back. Send me back! Now!" protested Tantri. But Hoki had already slammed the bedroom door shut behind her.

Back in the past, the villagers were shocked to see the vanishing act of their saviour, Tantri. But now that he was gone, they promptly chose Chief Tooja to become the king of their newly formed kingdom. Ironically, Chief Tooja decided to name the kingdom 'Hujli' in honour of their saviour – Tantri.

IN CINEMAPUR

It had been a long and arduous week at Hujli Palace with the visit of the ambassador from the Kingdom of Bijli. Raja Hooja had tasked his loyal minister, Tantri the Mantri, with the duty of entertaining the royal guests. Alas, the guests had been annoying, constantly demanding special treatment and generally getting on Tantri's nerves.

The day the ambassador had departed, Tantri decided to indulge in some self-care and made his way to the market, to his barber.

Ugh! I simply cannot suffer these fools anymore... I need a foolproof plan to take my rightful place as the king of Hujli, thought Tantri, as he leaned back in the barber's chair. *Perhaps, I can scheme with some like-minded inventive soul who believes in my genius... hmm... who could I work with?* Tantri pondered, as he stepped out of the hairdressing salon.

Deep in this thought, Tantri walked past the newspaper stand when a news article caught his eye...

Geet Dagal, one of Cinemapur's most celebrated and successful directors, is now in Hujli in search of a brand-new face for her latest movie! Auditions open to all.

Hmm... Interesting... thought Tantri absent-mindedly, when he noticed a large poster next to a cafe which read...

10 sure shot ways to get rid of your boss!

Meanwhile, just across the street a lady was handing over some photographs to a bespectacled man and speaking very animatedly.

"No, no, Amar. These don't work at all. None of them have any spunk. I am looking for some zing, some zest, some pizzazz! These are just too mundane. The main lead needs to stand out. Please, go look harder," Geet Dagal instructed her assistant.

"Casting for a movie can be so tiresome. I

need a coffee!" muttered Geet under her breath. As she crossed the road and made her way towards a cafe, an interesting shape caught her eye.

Geet noticed a man wearing a rather large turban, peering at some poster, unblinkingly. His sharp jawline, pointy nose and flamboyant moustache gave his personality a rare flourish... just the kind Geet had been searching for. "That's him! He would be perfect for my movie!" she exclaimed and approached him, "Excuse me, gentleman!"

"Yes?" asked Tantri, looking startled.

"Hello. My name is Geet Dagal and I am a film director from Cinemapur. May I know who you are?" asked Geet, cheerily.

"You certainly may. I am Hujli's most important person. I am none other than..."

But before Tantri could complete his introduction, Geet interrupted him, "Oh my! Raja Hooja himself. What an honour, Your Majesty!" She greeted him enthusiastically.

"Errr... I am the second-most important person — Tantri the Mantri, Raja Hooja's trusted minister," corrected Tantri. *But soon-to-be the mighty ruler of Hujli!* thought Tantri.

"Oh! That's even better! Because you, my dear Sir, are going to be the star of my next movie!" declared Geet, cheerfully.

"Who? What movie? No. I am not interested," said Tantri, dismissing the offer.

"But Tantriji, this is not just any part... it is the role of a lifetime!" exclaimed Geet.

"No, thank you! I am too busy for this!" declined Tantri, while thinking, *the only role I have my eyes set on is that of the king*.

Geet Dagal was not just a talented film-maker but also a keen observer. She had noticed the contents of the poster that Tantri had been reading earlier.

"Of course, you must be very busy focussing on your goal. But it is not going to be easy to become king," said Geet, having made a reasonable conclusion.

"Huh? What? How do you know about..." Tantri's voice trailed off, as he realised that he had let the cat out of the bag.

As Tantri started to walk away, Geet added slyly, "It's completely understandable... A cat always wants to be a lion and a Mantri will always want to be king. In fact, Mantriji, I think I can even help you achieve this goal. All you need to do is say 'yes' to..."

"Yes, absolutely yes!" replied Tantri.

"Perfect! So, you are the star of my latest

action movie 'Once Upon a Time,'" stated Geet, triumphantly.

"Wait! What? No... I meant 'yes' to become king," protested Tantri.

"Starring in my film will be the stepping stone to the throne of Hujli," explained Geet.

"I am confused. How will acting in your film help me become king?" asked Tantri, curiously.

"Just imagine... a world where every road has massive hoardings of you looking heroic... every newspaper is singing your praises... every child wants your autograph... every adult idolises you... and every kingdom wants you to be their king!" Geet painted a rosy picture of Tantri's glorious future.

Listening to her words, Tantri had drifted into a daydream where his subjects were chanting his name, while he sat snugly on his royal throne.

Tantri had a dreamy look in his eyes and Geet knew she had captured his interest.

"So, you see, as I was saying, once you star in my film, people will get to see you in a brand-new avatar... not Tantri the ordinary Mantri... but Tantri the extraordinary leader who is fearless and ready to do anything to save his kingdom!"

"Yes... Tantri for king!" added Tantri, happily.

"You will be seen as a larger-than-life, brave and strong hero, swinging into action

to help his people!" exaggerated Geet, with outstretched arms.

"Umm... but that's not the 'real' me. People will know that's just a character I am playing, right?" asked Tantri, seeming unsure.

"Well, most people cannot tell the difference between 'real' and 'reel'. They tend to believe what they see on the big screen as

the truth. Trust me, I have been in the show business for over two decades," assured Geet. "So, what do you say, Mantriji?

"Let's do it! It's worth a shot," agreed Tantri. *It's not like I have any other backup plan to get rid of that annoying Hooja at the moment*, he thought.

A few weeks later, an excited Tantri made his way to the glitz and glamour of the famous film city - Cinemapur. He was given a luxurious vanity van and assigned an assistant. A whole team of make-up and hair artists fussed over him all day long. The film crew treated Tantri the Mantri like royalty.

I could get used to this. It's good practice for when I become the king, he thought.

The shoot began and it turned out that Tantri was a natural in front of the camera. All the years of pretending to be loyal and agreeable in front of Raja Hooja had finally paid off.

He was effortless at faking emotions and his 'never give up' attitude helped him ace the action sequences. It didn't take long for him to find his footing, given all the special treatment that came his way.

One day, Geet and her team were shooting a difficult action scene with Tantri dangling from a rope hanging off the high ceiling, on the set.

"So Tantri, all you need to do is smoothly scale down the castle, look towards the camera and shout 'attack', okay?" Geet instructed. "Lights, Camera, Action!"

But instead of saying attack, Tantri pointed away from the camera and screamed, "Hooja!"

"No, no, no, not Hooja! Your line is 'Attack'. Let's try again," said Geet, while wondering, *Can this man ever not think about Hooja?*

"Lights, Camera, Act..."

"No, no, no! Look! Hooja!" yelled Tantri, as he pointed behind a baffled-looking Geet. "Welcome Your Highness."

"Oh, great!" replied Geet, half-heartedly looking at the king of Hujli strutting towards them. *I wonder what Raja Hooja is doing here*, she thought.

Tantri promptly slid down and took off his safety gear. He looked eager to meet his king, while secretly wishing Hooja would electrocute himself on some electric wire and vanish forever.

"What a pleasant surprise, Your Majesty! How kind of you to drop by," said Tantri. *Typical Hooja, always trying to steal my thunder! This is literally my spotlight,* sulking inwardly.

"Oh, my dear Tantri! I have missed you dearly. So, instead of summoning you to the palace, I thought I would come to see you myself in Cinemapur," said Raja Hooja, giving his favourite minister a hug.

"How thoughtful," smiled Tantri, as he rolled his eyes.

Geet noticed how Tantri's demeanour had changed on the king's arrival. She realised that having Hooja on the set would only distract Tantri and delay their shoot.

"Welcome to Cinemapur, Your Highness. So nice of you to grace us with your presence. I was wondering if I could speak to you in private," requested Geet.

Geet led Raja Hooja to her office space and offered him some refreshments and sweets. Food always put Raja Hooja in a good mood. Once he had relished the laddoos, Geet smartly placed forth her request.

"It's so wonderful for Your Royal Highness to come here himself to boost the morale of his trusted Mantri. Tantri is such a talented actor, but I fear that with you here, he might feel self-conscious and get distracted from his work," explained Geet.

"Oh yes, yes! That's true. Tantri thinks very highly of me. My opinion matters a lot to him," agreed Raja Hooja.

"Yes, of course! So... I was wondering if you would be kind enough to wait here in my office till the shot is over. That way, Tantri won't lose focus and we can wrap up the scenes swiftly," added Geet.

"Of course. Anything for my dear Tantri!" said the king, merrily.

Geet showed Raja Hooja her personal mini fridge full of tasty snacks. She thanked him for his generous cooperation and returned to the set.

But soon it was lunch time and Raja Hooja got restless. The snacks were good but not nearly as filling. He had heard that the food served on film sets was quite delicious and decided to find his way to the lunch room. Raja Hooja wandered down the corridor and found a door labelled 'Special'.

"Ah... this must be it! What else is more special than food?" said Raja Hooja to himself.

But the king was mistaken. He had entered into a room full of colourful buttons with lights and some levers. Instead of leaving, Raja Hooja started pressing the buttons randomly and tugging at the levers.

"Maybe this will summon someone with my lunch," wondered Raja Hooja, aloud.

Meanwhile, on the set there was absolute havoc. Sandbags were falling from the ceiling, trapdoors were opening and shutting furiously and firecrackers were going off without warning. The crew and the actors were running helter-skelter and screaming at each other.

"Run! Run!"

"Get away from the firecrackers!"

BOOM! CRASH! BANG!

"Watch out, Tantri!" warned Geet, but it was too late. Tantri lay in a heap, crushed under a sandbag and blasted by the firecrackers.

"Can someone please find out who is in the special effects room? Hurry! Make this stop, right now!" commanded Geet.

She ran to help poor Tantri, who was mumbling, "Tantri the hero... Tantri the king!"

"Amar, quickly call for an ambulance!" Geet instructed her assistant.

Meanwhile, the clueless king kept pushing some more buttons, but since no one appeared with a tray of food, he left the room and returned to the set. The place looked empty and in shambles.

"Is the shoot done? Where is everyone? At the lunchroom?" asked Raja Hooja, eagerly.

A staff member informed Raja Hooja of the series of events and how their lead actor was badly injured and rushed to the hospital.

"Oh! Movie sets can be so unpredictable. My poor Tantri! I must go see him immediately," said Raja Hooja, oblivious to the part he had played in his minister's fate.

At the hospital, the doctor made a thorough examination of Tantri's injuries and informed Geet about his medical diagnoses.

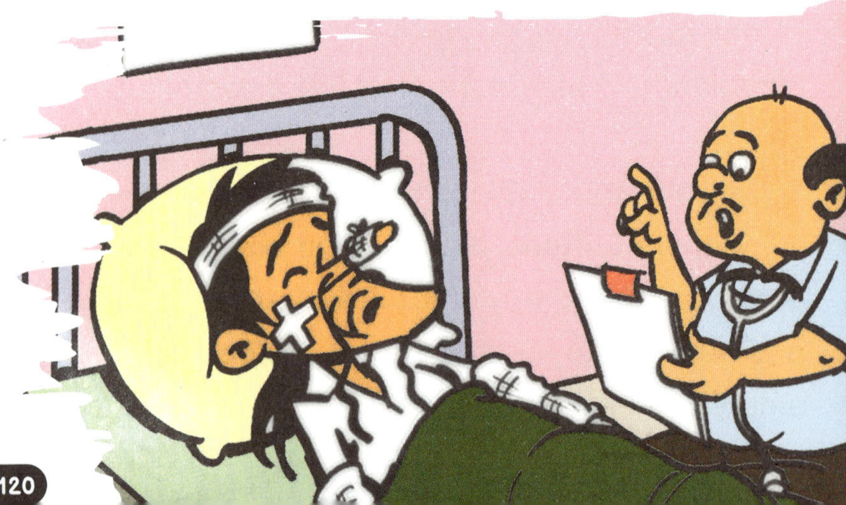

"This does not look good. Tantriji has multiple fractures in his arms and legs. His head is badly bruised and he most likely has a concussion. We will have to wait for him to be fully conscious to check. Also, his blood pressure is at an all-time high. He is going to need at least five months to rest and fully recover."

"Five months! That's way too long! How will I shoot my movie?" asked Geet, selfishly.

Just then, Raja Hooja burst in and cried, "Oh, my dearest friend! I came here as soon as I heard about your terrible accident."

Ugh! What is Hooja doing here? Even in the hospital it's hard to find a moment's peace, sighed Tantri, through his drowsy stupor. Looking at Raja Hooja's dramatic outburst, Geet had an idea.

"Your Majesty, may I have a word with you in private?" requested Geet, sweetly.

While Tantri sensed something was off, he was in too much pain to protest and just resigned himself to his fate.

One morning, a few months later, while Tantri

continued his recovery at the hospital, a nurse walked in and greeted him. For once Tantri wasn't brooding and had woken up in a good mood. The room was dim, and so he asked the nurse to open the blinds to let some sunshine in.

But when she rolled up the blinds, Tantri saw a massive hoarding of a new movie... not just any movie, but the one he was to star in. To his utter horror, it now starred his arch nemesis — Raja Hooja!

"Argh! Hoojaaaaa! One day soon, I will make sure your 'movie' ends forever!"

ABOUT

TINKLE

Tinkle has been entertaining children across the ages for more than forty-two years. With its unique combination of comic stories and factoids, Tinkle is that wonderful place where learning meets fun.

Tinkle is also home to some of India's most iconic cartoon characters like Shikari Shambu, Suppandi and Tantri the Mantri. Over the years, a bunch of younger toons have joined them in Tinkle Town, such as the Defective Detectives, WingStar, Ina, Mina, Mynah, Mo, and NOIS.

ABOUT

Being one of the oldest publishing houses in India, Rupa has been in the business of storytelling for more than eight decades. And with our collaboration with Tinkle, we have turned younger! Our success is due to our loyal base of authors and readers as well as teamwork and dedication of all at Rupa. Providing a wide selection of books that entertain, engage, move and delight, we remain at the forefront of storytelling in India, and a house for bestsellers.